Prayers:
Praying God's Word

By Gloria M. Fustino

Prayer Journal Included

Xulon
PRESS

To Paul & Judy,

God bless you always

With love & Blessings

Gloria

John 15:7-8

Acknowledgements

I want to thank my daughter Rita and my son Joe
for all their prayers, encouragement, input and
help in reviewing this work.
I especially want to thank Joan Stombres for assistance with the
technical side of this work and a big thanks to Carmen Pelaez for
her assistance with photographs.
More than anyone I want to thank and praise my Lord and Savior
Jesus Christ for saving me, filling me, teaching, leading and
guiding me along the path He has ordained for me.

Table of Contents

"And when you pray, do not heap up phrases (multiply words, repeating the same ones over and over) as the Gentiles do, for they think they will be heard for their much speaking. Do not be like them, for your Father knows what you need before you ask Him. Pray, therefore, like this: Our Father Who is in heaven, hallowed (kept holy) be your name. Your kingdom come, your will be done on earth as it is in heaven. Give us this day our daily bread. And forgive us our debts, as we also have forgiven (left, remitted, and let go of the debts, and have given up resentment against) our debtors. And lead (bring) us not into temptation, But deliver us from the evil one. For yours is the kingdom and the power and the glory forever. Amen." Matthew 6:7-13 (Amplified)

ASK AND YOU WILL RECEIVE

❊

J esus taught us how to pray and gave us the example in Matthew 6:7-13 (Amplified) Jesus said that "your Father knows what you need before you ask." "So when you ask," He said to "pray like this;" pray in this manner. It wasn't to be a prayer by rote; it was to be a prayer from your heart to your Heavenly Father. You can pray this prayer because you memorized it and it is written in your heart but it must be with an acknowledgement and understanding of what you are praying. "Our Father in heaven, hallowed be thy name;" He is showing us that we are to approach our Heavenly Father with respect and reverence. The word *hallowed* is to acknowledge that He is holy and to be honored and revered. By doing this we are first praising and honoring Him for who He is and then declaring our commitment and submission to His Kingdom to come and His will to be done on earth as it is in Heaven. Next you may ask for your daily needs followed by asking for his forgiveness just as you forgive those who have hurt you. This is the requirement for all praying: we forgive as he forgives us. Jesus continues teaching us how to pray by declaring that we can trust and look to our father in heaven to deliver us from evil. As you go through the scriptures let the Holy Spirit give you light concerning His instruction in it. This was to be our pattern for prayer.

For our purposes of praying God's word, I draw your attention to the portion of this prayer that says, "Thy will be done on earth as it is in heaven." How do you know what His will is? You can know His will from the Word of God. His Will is His Word. As you study and meditate on the Word of God the Holy Spirit begins to reveal to you what the Will of God is concerning your needs. If you are not sure God wants to bless you with finances or other provision, or not sure if He wants to heal you, then you will not be able to pray with confidence. That's why you must seek Him in His Word; find His will and pray according to the Word of God. Then you will know you are praying in His will.

Do you know that God cannot do anything for us unless we ask? Think about it. Jesus said our Father knows what we have need of before we ask, but continues to teach us to ask and how to ask. There are many references requiring us to ask throughout the whole Bible. We can't assume because we have accepted Christ as our Savior that God will just take care of everything apart from us. Yes, He does know what we have need of, but He continually teaches us in the Word to "ask." Our part is to ask and to ask according to His Word. John 15:7 says "If you abide in me and my words abide in you, you shall ask what you will and it shall be done unto you." When you abide, spend time with, meditate on His Word, you will know how to pray according to the Will of God and you can ask and it shall be done. It doesn't get done until you ask. It is the prayer of faith that raises the sick, but it is the asking for that healing and believing because you know it is the Will of God. The Bible teaches to ask and you shall receive, call to Him and He will hear and answer. When you seek Him you will find Him. Men "ought always to pray and not turn coward (faint, lose heart, and give up)" (Luke 18:1 Amplified), because if you're praying according to His Word, you will be encouraged, not discouraged, and you will be asking as he requires. Prayer is asking and you ask because you believe He will do it. You are asking in faith, because you trust Him, knowing His will and believing what you can't see until it comes to pass. James says in chapter 4:2, that you "have not because you ask not" and sometimes you don't receive because you asked incorrectly and with wrong motives.

Reading this book and then studying and meditating on the scriptures will give you insight and simple steps on how to incorporate the Word of God into your prayers making it easier to include them into your daily routine. As you do this you will find yourself praying in accordance with God's Word and you will receive His full blessings. Sometimes we pray and wonder why or what God wants from us. These scriptures combined in prayer will lead to the answers you are seeking. The Holy Spirit will make it real to you.

HOW TO PRAY AND GET RESULTS

In Isaiah 55:8 God tells us "For my thoughts are not your thoughts, neither are your ways my ways, saith the LORD. For as the heavens are higher than the earth, so are my ways higher than your ways, and my thoughts than your thoughts." His ways and thoughts are higher than ours. You can't out-do God; you can't out give God; you can't create anything or make any changes without God, but if you are in Christ, then you have the mind of Christ and able to know God's plan for your situation. As long as you obey the Lord then those things that God speaks to your heart will come to pass. Sometimes you have ideas on how to get something done; how to make changes that are necessary, but you must first seek Him and His way and then you must obey. God may require something of you, maybe making a move or a change in your life that you are not sure you want to do, and you want to be obedient to Him. Maybe you don't have a habit of prayer every day, so the first step for you is just making time to pray every day. You do it out of obedience and you trust Him knowing He is leading you to a higher place in Him. Commit to Him and obey. God has set the course, His Word will go forth out of His mouth and it will not return to Him empty (or void), but it will accomplish and prosper according to what it was sent forth to do. So if you pray according to the Word of God and the Will of God concerning your life, you know and can trust Him that His Words that you speak and believe will come to pass…it will not return void. Though you may find yourself uncomfortable and hesitant to act, because of His Word you can trust Him and have faith that He is taking care of you; that He is leading you. You must learn to pray according to the Word of God. I do that by taking the Word that pertains to my request and make it my prayer; thus I am praying His Word and His will. As you do this, there will be times when you have something that needs prayer and the Holy Spirit will bring a scripture to your remembrance. As you follow the leading of the Holy Spirit and the Word of God He has brought to you, this will develop into the perfect prayer for your situation.

WHEN TO PRAY

D on't let the troubles of the day, whether it's personal, political or otherwise, cause you to get stressful and worried. Things start coming at us the minute we wake up; the phone rings with something you weren't prepared for; the spouse, children or the boss is in a bad mood, but you can stay in faith. You, as a child of God and joint-heir with Christ, can stand above all of them. You must focus on Him and His Word. In Luke 18:1 Jesus said" Men ought always to pray and not faint (not give up)." Again, focus on Him and keep your mind set on Him, not on the problems. If you pray the problem you won't get anywhere; it is a robber of your faith in God because you don't get anything out of those kinds of prayers; nothing gets answered and then you want to blame God. Don't whine and ask God to fix this or that, but instead look to Him. Put the problem before Him, He knows what it is anyway, but you need to ask Him what Word covers this situation and commit it to Him by prayer and supplication. Pray the answer which is based on the Word of God. Paul said in Ephesians 6:18 (Amplified) "Pray at all times – on every occasion, in every season – in the Spirit with all (manner of) prayer and entreaty…" All manner of prayer means there are many ways to pray. Every moment that comes your way throughout your day should be used to rejoice, pray and listen for God to speak. You can pray anytime and anywhere; in your car, in the shower or riding in an elevator. I'm sure you get this point. If you think about it, you worry no matter where you are at any time and any place. No exceptions! So why can't you change the focus to your Lord and let Him do the work in and through you?

Paul said pray at all times with all manner of prayer. In this book we are specifically studying praying God's Word. To learn all about prayer is another teaching too large for this book. However, I will list some of the ways to pray and hope you will be moved to learn more. Included in praying the Word in your own language, there is: the prayer of binding and loosing; the prayer of agreement; the prayer of faith; the prayer of petition and supplication; the prayer of thanksgiving. I can't say this enough, but praise and worship is part of your thanksgiving communication and fellowship with God and helps you focus on Him in the midst of anything. Also in this list is the prayer of consecration and dedication; the prayer of commitment (again all these must always be based on the Word of God), and last but not least, is intercession which may be in your own language but also involves praying in the Spirit, which is in other tongues. Paul teaches in 1 Corinthians 14:2 "For he that speaks in an unknown tongue speaks not to men but to God; for no man understands him; howbeit in the spirit he speaks mysteries," and in 1 Corinthians 14:14 "If I pray in an unknown tongue, my spirit prays but my understanding (my mind, will and emotions; my intellect) is unfruitful." I pray that you will seek more understanding of prayer because it is the avenue by which all things will be done "on earth as it is in heaven."

MAKING PRAYER A DAILY ROUTINE

P rayer must be a way of life not just when you are in need. Prayer, praise and worship are what helps you focus on His provision instead of on the problem. Exalt Him above all else and place your complete trust and faith in Him. We all do it; we spend more time thinking and stressing about the problem. That's when we must "arrest" ourselves and turn our hearts and thoughts toward Him. You should always be in an attitude of prayer. That doesn't mean you have to stop everything you are doing. You can pray as you go all day long in between your work and other activities. However, you still must dedicate a portion of your time every day exclusively to Him and when you leave the prayer place you can take those promises of God with you to sustain you and keep you on even keel; no wavering like the wind-tossed sea. When the thought of the problem comes, speak those Words of promise and focus on them. Let them steady you in the storm; in the onslaught of the enemy when he comes with doubt and unbelief. Just say no! "I believe God, He is working it out for me and I trust Him, not the circumstances!"

INTERCEDING

※

S ometimes, in fact, many times your prayers are for others and not for yourself. Intercessory prayer is standing in the gap for someone else. You are the bridge that fills the gap on behalf of others. Again you can pray the Word regarding the situation or you can pray in the Spirit as the Lord leads you. There are times when you will first pray in the Spirit because you don't know how to pray for the person or situation. And after praying in the Spirit, the Lord will give you Words to pray according to His Will. As He teaches us in Romans 8:26 - 27 "It is the Holy Spirit Himself who helps you to pray when you don't know what to pray." He helps you to pray according to the will of God. The Holy Spirit helps or "takes hold together with you against your infirmities" which is your weakness, indicating inability to produce results. You don't know how to get the results you need. It is a weakness of yours. The Holy Spirit wants to help you with that. You may find yourself groaning and moaning when you pray. That is what is called travail in the Spirit. It is giving birth. "For we know not what we should pray for as we ought, but the Spirit Himself makes intercession for us with groanings which cannot be uttered." Groanings defined here means inarticulate speech in a language that you don't know. The scripture says "he searches the hearts and knows what the mind of the Spirit is because he makes intercession for the saints according to the will of God." Yes, the Holy Spirit takes hold together **with you** against your weakness and inability to produce results and gives you "groanings" or a way to express something in the Spirit; prayers that cannot be uttered! He will join with you to make intercession for the saints according to the Will of God. Romans 8:27 (Amplified) reads this way, "And He Who searches the hearts of men knows what is in the mind of the Holy Spirit – what His intent is because the Spirit intercedes and pleads before God in behalf of the saints according to and in harmony with God's will." Paul exhorts in 1 Timothy 2:1 "that first of all supplications, prayers, intercessions, and giving of thanks be made for all men...so that we may lead a quiet and peaceable life in all godliness and honesty." He talks again about travail in Galatians 4:19. Paul said he travails again so that Christ will be formed in us. When you get saved it is only the beginning and it takes your diligence in the Word, your prayers, and the prayers of others so that not only have you become born again but that you will grow into the image of Christ our Savior.

Jesus is always our example in groaning, weeping and travail. Because He is our example, we shouldn't have a problem with this type of prayer.

"When Jesus therefore saw her weeping, and the Jews also weeping which came with her, **he groaned in the spirit**, and was troubled, and said, where have ye laid him? They said unto him, Lord, come and see. **Jesus wept**. Then said the Jews, Behold how he loved him! And some of them said, Could not this man, which opened the eyes of the blind, have caused that even this man should not have died? **Jesus therefore again groaning in himself** cometh to the grave. It was a cave, and a stone lay upon it. Jesus said, Take ye away the stone. Martha, the sister of him that was dead, saith unto him, Lord, by this time he stinketh: for he hath been dead four days. Jesus saith unto her, Said I not unto thee, that, if thou wouldest believe, thou shouldest see the glory of God? Then they took away the stone from the place where the dead was laid. And Jesus lifted up his eyes, and said, **Father, I thank thee that thou hast heard me. And I knew that thou hearest me always: but because of the people which stand by I said it, that they may believe that thou hast sent me.** And when he thus had spoken, he cried with a loud voice, Lazarus, come forth. And he that was dead came forth, bound hand and foot with graveclothes: and his face was bound about with a napkin. Jesus saith unto them, Loose him, and let him go." (John 11:33-44)

In this portion of scripture you find that Jesus groaned in the spirit (verse 33) and in verse 35 it tells you that Jesus wept. He was not weeping because He didn't have the answer because He did. Again in verse 38 it says Jesus *groaned* in Himself. The result of the weeping, crying and groaning was that He raised Lazarus from the dead. God showed Him what to do and He did it. He admonished

Martha that if she would believe she would see the glory of God. Then they rolled the stone away and Jesus lifted up His eyes toward Heaven and thanked the Father that He had heard him. Think about that for a minute. When did Father hear Him? He heard Him when He wept; when He groaned in the Spirit. He knew that Father heard Him in the Spirit, but for the sake of the people He was speaking out loud for them to hear and believe. Then He spoke, "Lazarus come forth," and he did!

In Luke 19:41 you will see that Jesus wept over Jerusalem. And again in Hebrews 5:7 you will find Jesus offered up prayers and supplication with strong crying and tears. The difference is that He was feeling compassion and moved by the Holy Spirit. We, on the other hand, are many times moved by our own feelings and we cry for ourselves. Not that you shouldn't cry, but let's turn them into prayer. Let the compassion of God take over. A quick prayer here is: "Lord take my tears, take my groanings and hear me O Lord as I look to you and believe you for the answer." As God promised in His Word, He will turn our mourning in to joy and give us beauty for ashes.

Intercessory prayer is standing in the gap for others. Let me try to give you a picture of this. Someone is walking up the mountain trail; they come to the end and there is a chasm between them and the other side of the mountain. This is just like the chasm between us and God before we accepted Christ as our Savior. The other side is where they need to be to obtain their provision. Intercessory prayer is building a bridge, standing in the gap between their side and the other side so that they may cross over and attain what they need. We do pray intercessory prayer for ourselves, but mainly it is a prayer prayed for others. When you don't know how to pray for a certain person or situation you depend on the Holy Spirit to lead you by the Word, intercessions, travail, and weeping to bridge the gap for the person in need.

There are many scriptures that we can pray. Throughout the next pages you will find examples of prayers based on scripture that were quickened to my heart by the Holy Spirit as I sought the Lord. You can start with these, but let the Holy Spirit lead you to the perfect prayer and Word for you and yours. You want to pray correctly according to the Will of God so your prayer must be based on His Word. Your first commitment is to put the Word of God first place in your life. Proverbs 4:20-23 (Amplified) is a life scripture for me and should be for you too:

"Attend to my words; consent and submit to my sayings. Let them not depart from your sight; keep them in the center of your heart. For they (His Words) are life to those who find them, healing and health to all their flesh. Keep and guard your heart with all vigilance and above all that you guard, for out of it flow the springs of life."

Vigilant means to be attentive, watchful, observant and alert. If someone gives you advice about anything and you are not sure about it, your question to them should be, "What scripture is that based on?" You want to always stay in the parameters of the Word of God. Don't let the little foxes spoil the vine. Commit everything to prayer and let the Holy Spirit give you the revelation you need. Keep the Word first place in all things.

NOTHING IS TOO DIFFICULT FOR GOD

❄

G od tells us in Jeremiah 32:17 that there is "nothing too hard" for Him. In Jeremiah 33:3 He said "Call unto me, and I will answer thee and show thee great and mighty things, which thou knowest not." So we must call to Him and expect His answer. He didn't say maybe He WILL answer. He said He will answer and He will show you great and mighty things, which you do not know. He will show you things you need to know so you can pray effectively

Prayer:

Father, I have this need (you can tell him even though he already knows) and I don't know what to do. You said to call. So I am calling to you. Even though it seems impossible to me, I know nothing is impossible with You, Lord and nothing is too hard for you. I believe Your Word and when I call I know you will answer; you will show me things I do not know; things that are hidden that you will reveal to me. You will cause me to recognize and understand the knowledge of God; things that will show me how to proceed in my situation because I need to know what to do next. I thank You Lord that you hear me when I call and that I have ears to hear you answer. In Jesus' Name I pray.

LIKE A TREE PLANTED BY THE WATER

❈

Jeremiah 17:7-8 – "Blessed is the man that trusts in the Lord and whose hope the Lord is. For he shall be as a tree planted by the waters, and that spreads out her roots by the river, and shall not see when heat comes but her leaf shall be green; and shall not be careful in the year of drought, neither shall cease from yielding fruit."

Psalm 1:1-3 – "Blessed is the man that walks not in the counsel of the ungodly, nor stands in the way of sinners, nor sits in the seat of the scornful. But his delight is in the law of the LORD; and in his law doth he meditate day and night. And he shall be like a tree planted by the rivers of water, that brings forth his fruit in his season; his leaf also shall not wither; and whatsoever he does shall prosper."

John 15:16 – "You have not chosen me but I have chosen you and ordained you, that you should go and bring forth fruit, and that your fruit should remain: that whatsoever you shall ask of the Father in my name, He may give it you."

Y ou want to be strong in Him, like a tree planted by the waters. Think about that for a minute. There is a place where I used to live and there were trees lined up along the water's edge. They never seemed to fade nor wither. They withstood the heat of the summer, storms, cold winters with snow and ice and they were still standing strong and producing buds in the spring and then the leaves as God intended. Those trees were in the right place, just like you must be in a place to be blessed. You must not take heed to the scorners or the ungodly...they don't know what they are talking about; they don't know God. For a moment they don't see any fruit, they only see bare limbs; but, they don't know what we know. In Jeremiah 17:7-8 and Psalm 1:1-3 you are taught that you will be like that tree, who is getting its nourishment and strength from the water, just as you are to stand strong and receive nourishment from the Water of God's Word. Then as you meditate on the Word, you will conduct yourselves appropriately and your faith will be built to believe. You will bring forth fruit in his season and your fruit will not wither and whatever you do shall prosper. You won't have to be afraid of the heat or the famine.

John 15:16 reminds you that He has chosen you and ordained you to bring forth fruit and that your fruit would continue to bear more fruit and He said your fruit should remain...it will last and because of that, you can ask the Father anything in the Name of Jesus and He will give it to you.

Prayer:

Father, I am blessed because my trust and hope is in you. I thank you that you have chosen me and that you have ordained that I should bring forth fruit in its season. Even though I am facing certain situations in my life I trust you. I do not fellowship among the ungodly, the sinners and scorners, but my delight is in You Lord and in Your Word. I look to you and not to the world for my answers. I will be strong like a tree that is planted by the rivers of water. My roots go deep into the water of God's Holy Word. I will bring forth fruit in its season. I know you hear and answer my prayers. Nothing I do will wither or fade and whatever I do will prosper. Because I stay in the Word and meditate on it, I will not see when the heat of the day (the problems) come but I will flourish through the heat and even in lack I will not cease from yielding fruit and my fruit shall remain. In Jesus' Name I pray.

WRITE THE WORD UPON YOUR HEART

T here are several places in the Bible that talk about writing the Word upon our hearts. In Jeremiah he speaks of it and the promise that comes with it; that when you write the Word in your heart (by studying and meditating) He will demonstrate His love to you.

He loves you so much that he chooses to forgive all of your iniquity. Not only that, he will not remember them again. The only way it is remembered again is when it comes to your thought life by the enemy of your soul to remind you how bad you are and about all your failures; but you can look to Him in his Word and you can know you are God's forgiven people because you accepted Jesus as your Lord and Savior; you are now forgiven and made the righteousness of God in Christ Jesus.

> Jeremiah 31:33-34 – "I will put my law in their inward parts, and write it in their hearts; and will be their God and they shall be my people.....for I will forgive their iniquity, and I will remember their sin no more."

Prayer:

Lord, as I spend time in Your Word and I meditate on it, your Word is being written in my heart, I am yours. Though I am not perfect, I have the Perfect One in me, my Lord Jesus Christ. You have forgiven all my iniquities and have thrown them as far as the east is from the west. That is infinity, never to meet, and according to your Word you do not remember my sin anymore. I thank you Lord for cleansing me and receiving me into your arms again. Because I believe you I know you hear me when I call and will answer my prayers. I know the problems that I face today will be resolved. In Jesus' Name I pray. Amen!

BE STRONG AND VERY COURAGEOUS

❊

I n Joshua chapter 1, we learn that we are to be strong and very courageous. We are to stay on the straight and narrow path not turning to the right or to the left, because when we obey this command, we ourselves will make our way prosperous and will deal wisely and we will have good success wherever we go. That is His promise to you. You put His Word first place in your life, you hear from Him; you act on it and it comes to pass as it is written. You must meditate on the Word of God day and night and then He will give you revelation of what it means. You will see and then do the Word of God. He says "observe to do according to all that is written" that means you will "see" and then you must act on it, then you will make your way prosperous and you will have good success. What a promise, but in receiving it you must be strong and of good courage. Don't let fear or dismay come in. "God has not given you a spirit of fear, but of power and love and a sound mind and discipline and self-control." (2 Tim 1:7 Amplified) And He has promised "never to leave you nor forsake you." (Hebrews 13:5)

Joshua 1:7-9 – "Only be strong and very courageous, **that you may observe to do** according to all the law, which

Moses my servant commanded thee: turn not from it to the right hand or to the left that you may prosper wherever you go. This book of the law shall not depart out of your mouth; but you shall meditate therein day and night, **that you may observe to do** according to all that is written therein: for then you shall make your way prosperous, and then you shall have good success. Have not I commanded you? Be strong and of a good courage; be not afraid, neither be thou dismayed: for the LORD your God is with you wherever you go."

Prayer:

I commit to being a doer of the word; I am strong and very courageous. I will speak the Word and meditate on it day and night and because of that I will see (observe, grasp and understand) what the Lord is instructing me to do and I will do it. I will prosper where ever I go because I will not turn from His way to the right hand or to the left. This Word of God shall not depart out of my mouth; but I will meditate on it day and night, so that I will see what to do according to all that you have written. Because of this commitment to you Lord, I will make my way prosperous, and I will have good success according to Your Word. I thank You Lord that you are with me wherever I go; that you are leading me and guiding me in all my decisions. In Jesus' Name I pray. Amen.

HIS THOUGHTS & PLANS FOR ME

J ust as loving parents have good thoughts toward their children, our Father has good thoughts toward us. They are thoughts of peace and not of evil. Remember God is the Father of all. He wanted us; He loves us and wants us to do well. Jeremiah said in chapter 29:11-12, "For I know the thoughts and plans that I have for you….thoughts and plans for welfare and peace and not for evil, to give you hope in your final outcome." Welfare is defined as well-being, happiness, safety, health and prosperity. Those are His thoughts and plans for us. Then He says we can call upon Him and pray to Him and He will hear and heed us. He is ready to hear and answer, but you must look to Him, talk to Him, and expect Him to hear and to answer. Jesus reinforced the message of supply by telling us in John 10:10 that the thief comes to steal, kill and de-stroy, but that He has come that we may have and enjoy life and have it in abundance, to the full, till it overflows. We must trust Him. Ask and receive that your joy may be full.

Prayer:
Lord God your thoughts and plans toward me are good and not evil. Thank you that you have plans to give me peace, a hope

and a future. Thank you for giving me life and blessings and not evil. I trust you for my well-being, happiness, safety, health and prosperity. Evil is from the thief and I resist him in the mighty Name of Jesus. I know that you want me to have an abundant life in you, doing your will, plans and purposes on the earth and I commit to your plan and receive your peace. In Jesus' Name I pray. Amen!

THE LORD IS MY SHEPHERD

✳

P salm 23:1 reminds us that God said He is our Shepherd and that we will not lack or want for any good thing. It is His wish, His will, "that above all things you would prosper and be in health even as your soul prospers." (3 John 2) So you must let the Word of God abide in you richly. Read it, study it, meditate on it and it will cause your mind, will and emotions to prosper in God and in so doing you will have good health. The more you renew your minds and learn the Word, the stronger you will get. Then the Word works in your spirit, soul and body bringing you to a place of peace and health because you can trust Him. Not only does he want you to prosper and be in health, but Proverbs 10:22 says "the blessing of the Lord makes us rich and He adds no sorrow with it." God is not giving with one hand and taking away with the other. He is a good God and Father and we want to demonstrate that by living our lives for Him, bringing glory to His Name. What better way to give glory to God than to let the world see that God is taking care of us no matter what, because we believe and trust Him?

The Lord our Shepherd has taught that what we sow, we shall reap. (Galatians 6:7) In Luke 6:38 it says that we should give and when we give, gifts will come back to us, given by men. Not only will the gifts come back to us; I heard it said this way: If you give someone a bushel of fruit, the blessing will come back not only the measure that was given, but it will be pressed down so that it fills every space in the bushel and then it will be shaken to make sure it all goes down in and fills every spot, and then more will be added to it until it overflows....that is, "good measure, pressed down and shaken together will men give into your bosom." We need to understand that the same way we give is same way we will receive. It's not just about giving natural fruit, it is about giving of ourselves and how we respond to others. As you ponder that thought make a decision to always be generous; looking to give more than you get, knowing He will always bless you abundantly.

Prayer:

Lord, thank You that it is your will for me to prosper and to be healthy and whole; and that you do not expect me to live in lack or want. So as I renew my mind to your Word you are blessing me continually. I thank you that it is not your will for me to be poor, but to be rich in all ways; that is enough to meet every need and then to give to the gospel and to help others. And as I obey your Word, you do not bring sorrow with your blessings. I thank you that as I am obedient in giving, your blessings flow to me and according to your plan you cause men to give to me. I will be a generous cheerful giver. I will not look to men, but to you Lord and I will keep my eyes on you. I un-

derstand that as I sow I will reap, so I will sow generously and accept your promise to expect the blessings to flow to me. Your word says you are "able to make all grace abound toward me so that I will always and under all circumstances and whatever the need, be self-sufficient having enough to require no aid or support, and that I will be furnished in abundance for every good work."(2 Cor. 9:8 Amplified) In Jesus' Name I receive all your blessings. Amen.

THE BLESSING OF TITHING

I n the beginning, as a new Christian, I didn't understand about tithing, but as I looked to the Holy Spirit, He has shown me that this is another promise that God our Father has put in place for our good. Obviously He doesn't need the money. He owns it all. This is for our benefit. We learned in the Old Testament according to Malachi 3:10 that we should bring our tithe into the storehouse; the storehouse is the place where we are fed. Leviticus 27:30-32 teaches us that the tithe belongs to the Lord and is holy (separated and dedicated) unto Him. When you tithe not only does it bring provision for you but it is also a blessing for the place where you are being fed spiritually. Our Father in heaven has promised that when you tithe, the windows of heaven will be opened for you and a blessing will be poured out upon you that you do not have room enough to receive it all. Think about that….the windows of heaven opened for us, pouring blessings upon us so much that we will not have enough room to receive them. Not only that, but He promised to rebuke the devourer for our sake. The devourer is the one who wants to destroy everything you put your hand to do. When you start something and before it gets to maturity it fails, that is the devourer and God said

He would rebuke the devourer for your sake if you tithe and consider it holy unto the Lord.

Tithing is a whole other teaching but for our purposes here we need to remember that Abraham tithed and that we are Abraham's seed and heirs of the promise made to him. Remember this was before the law was put in place. So tithing is before Moses and the law. Tithing is a way for our Father to bless us when we obey Him. Jesus also talked about the tithe. He mentioned in Luke 11:42 (Amplified) that they were tithing their mint and rue and every little herb but they disregarded the justice and love of God. Jesus Himself said, they ought to tithe but they should not leave off the commandment to love. They thought because they tithed they didn't have to love as God commanded and Jesus was correcting them. He was in no way doing away with the tithe.

The fruit of their ground supplied their purchasing power; it was like our money today. So Jesus did not do away with the tithe. He came to fulfill the law not destroy it. (Matt. 5:17) Money is our way of functioning in this world, so tithing our income is the means of obtaining the blessings of God as we obey Him. With the blessings of Abraham also come the requirements. So don't talk yourself out of tithing. Talk yourself into it. You will not be as blessed if you don't.

Prayer:

Father in Heaven, in obedience to Your Word, I bring my tithe into your storehouse where I receive my food (The Word of God) that sustains me. I thank you for all your blessings that you are pouring out on me and my house. I receive it and give back to you in obedience to Your Holy Spirit. Your blessings come up on me and overtake me. I thank you Father that you have already rebuked the devourer (satan, the enemy, the evil one) on my behalf so that all the fruits of my labor will come to maturity and not be destroyed. Nothing I put my hand to will fall to the ground, fade or wither because I am a tither and I am trusting in you. Thank You Lord! In Jesus' Name I pray.

GOD'S BOOK OF REMEMBRANCE

※

There is another scripture I read recently in Malachi 3:16-18 (Amplified) that touched my heart and I want to share it with you.

> Malachi 3:16-18 (Amplified)- "Then those who feared the Lord talked often one to another; and the Lord listened and heard it, and a book of remembrance was written before Him of those who reverenced and worshipfully feared the Lord and who thought on His name. And they shall be Mine, says the Lord of hosts, in that day when I publicly recognize and openly declare them to be My jewels (My special possession, My peculiar treasure). And I will spare them, as a man spares his own son who serves him. Then shall you return and discern between the righteous and the wicked, between him who serves God and him who does not serve Him."

We grew up knowing that God hears all, knows all, and sees all, but when I read this scripture somehow I understood even more the love of God as my Father. It isn't about Him recording all our bad words and thoughts (not that we didn't have them), but it is about Him wanting to remember and record those words and thoughts that bring glory and honor to Him. He is keeping us on the plus side. This scripture says that the Lord listened to those who reverenced and worshipfully feared the Lord and who thought on His Name. It says He even hears our thoughts; He listens as we speak about Him, as we testify of His goodness, and He hears it and puts it in a book of remembrance. It is written and recorded of all those who worship and reverently fear and honor the Lord by talking of Him to one another and testifying of His goodness and thinking on His Name. When I first committed my life to Christ, I went to a church that always had testimony time and since I've read this scripture I appreciate even more the time that the saints in this church took to testify of the Lord's goodness.

Writing a book of remembrance is something a lot of people do for their own family. Their children say something wonderful or they do something wonderful and the parents want to record it in a book with pictures or a video so that all could see. Well, that first came from God our Father. He said they shall be His and that one day He will publicly recognize and openly declare them to be His jewels, His special possession, and His peculiar treasure. (Malachi 3:17 Amplified) In 1 Peter 2:10 we are reminded that because of Jesus we are "a chosen generation, a royal priesthood, a holy nation, a peculiar people that should show forth the praises of Him who called us out of darkness and into His marvelous light." He loves when we praise Him and thank Him for bringing us into His family.

My heart leapt at the thought of what this scripture means because I saw how much He loves us. We love our children, our nieces and nephews and we are so proud of them when they accomplish something or say something good, and now you see that Our Father is the first proud Father. So when we honor Him and speak and think highly of Him, He writes them in a book of remembrance. Hallelujah!!!

Prayer:

Lord, keep a guard over my mouth and let me only speak those wonderful things you have done in my life. As I talk to others and testify of Your goodness to me and my house, I know You hear it and You put it in Your book of remembrance to make a note of who reverences and worshipfully fears and respects you. At one time I did not belong to you, but now I am a chosen generation, a royal priesthood, a holy nation, a peculiar people and because of Jesus My Lord, You have openly declared that I am your jewel, your special possession, your peculiar treasure and you will spare me from the works of the enemy. Thank You my dear Heavenly Father for taking care of me and for looking upon me and choosing me to be in your family!

DELIVERED TO THE BLESSINGS

I n Deuteronomy 28 we read about all the blessings that come from obeying God and the curses from disobedience. Then we learned that it was Christ who redeemed us from the curse that came under the law, and delivered us to the blessings of Abraham. We must be ever mindful of the facts spoken of in Galatians 3:13-14 and verse 29 that we are blessed because Jesus hung on the cross and died and was resurrected for us so that the blessing of Abraham would come on us through Jesus Christ and that we have now received the promise of the Holy Spirit through faith. Since we are Christ's, then we are redeemed from the curse.

Prayer:

Lord Jesus you have redeemed me from the curse of the law, being made a curse for me. You did this so that THE BLESSING of Abraham would come on me! I receive the promise of the Spirit through faith because I am Abraham's seed through Jesus and an heir according to this promise. All the promises of Abraham's Covenant are mine because I am the seed of Abraham through Christ Jesus. Thank You Lord that I am the head and not the tail; I am above only and not beneath.

The enemies that come against me one way will flee before me seven ways. The blessing of the Lord is upon my home, my family (including my children and children's children), my job and everything I put my hand to. We are blessed coming in and blessed going out. According to your Word, we shall have a surplus of prosperity. The Lord will open the heavens to give the rain in its season. The Lord will give us power to get wealth that He may establish His covenant in the earth. You have promised us prolonged life on this earth and a life worth living

I will study and meditate on all these blessings and share them with others, helping them to receive this promise. I thank you for the abundant provision you have made for me. In Jesus' Name I pray. Amen!

TAKE NO THOUGHT

❊

S ometimes we get into anxiety and stress just like the people of Jesus' day. He's speaking to us today as He did then; telling us not to take those thoughts concerning what we will eat and drink and where our clothes will come from.

> Matthew 6:31-34 (KJV) – "Therefore take no thought, saying, what shall we eat? Or, what shall we drink? Or, Wherewithal shall we be clothed? (For after all these things do the Gentiles seek); for your heavenly Father knows that you have need of all these things. But seek you first the kingdom of God, and his righteousness; and all these things shall be added unto you. Take therefore no thought for the morrow: for the morrow shall take thought for the things of itself. Sufficient unto the day is the evil thereof."

I find this interesting in view of the fact that even in Moses' day, when he led the children of Israel out of Egypt, while they were out in the wilderness; scripture says their clothes and shoes never wore out.

Deuteronomy 29:5 (Amplified) "I have led you forty years in the wilderness; your clothes have not worn out upon you, and your sandals have not worn off your feet."

Nehemiah 9:21 (Amplified) "Forty years you sustained them in the wilderness; they lacked nothing, their clothes did not wear out, and their feet did not swell."

Your heavenly Father knows you need a roof over your head, clothes and food to eat. He knows you have those needs and more. He admonishes us to seek not those things, but to seek first His kingdom and His righteousness. Seek Him first; put the Word of God first place in your life. It is already written, He will take care of those needs if we put Him first in all things. And don't worry about tomorrow, you have enough to take care of today. God will do that for you if you let him. So find your rest and peace in Him.

Prayer:

Father, I will seek you first. I will not worry or be fretful over what I need, but instead I seek first your kingdom and your way of doing and being right. I am confident Lord that you will supply all I need! Because of that, I will not fret or worry, but will rest in you knowing you are working on my behalf even though I don't see it or feel it, but because you said it in your

Word, I trust you. I know all provision will come. I will not lack or want for anything. Thank you Lord. In Jesus' Name I pray. Amen!

RUN TO HIM

I n James 4:7-8 you are reminded to submit yourselves to God and to resist the evil one, the devil, and when you resist him, he must flee from you. Then James reminds you to draw near to God and as you are drawing near to Him, He is drawing near to you. What a wonderful picture I have of running to my Heavenly Father and He with arms open is coming toward me. The Amplified bible says "Come close to God and He will come close to you." The enemy tries to come against us in many ways including family members, our finances, our jobs, our friends and more. We do not have to fear, we just come close to God, submit to Him, get in the Word, meditate on it day and night, write it on your heart and resist the devil in the powerful and mighty Name of the Lord Jesus Christ and he must flee. When trouble happens make up your mind you will run to your Heavenly Father. The devil tries to convince us there is no help in God, but don't listen to that voice. Run to your Heavenly Father; He is already there!

Prayer:

I am so grateful that you are my Father. I submit myself – including all my family, my finances, my job, my friends and

my home to you Lord God. I resist the devil and he must flee from me! I run to you my Heavenly Father and as I run to You, You are already drawing close to me. I can hardly fathom this great love you have for me. Oh thank you Father that you care so much for me!

TRUST IN GOD'S MERCY AND PROVISION

T he Psalms are clearly David's prayers to God. He always turned his thoughts and opened his soul to Him and poured out the things that were on his mind and heart. God is our Father, and just like David, we can have a talk with Him about everything and we should. No matter what he had on his mind, David always began by praising God and thanking Him for His goodness. An example is found in Psalm 13 when David felt like God had forgotten him. "How long will you forget me oh Lord?" How many times have we asked that same question? We think like David did; that the enemy is winning, but David declared his trust in God's mercy and abundant provision. He rejoices in God's salvation (and I love this part)…he declares his trust in the Lord; he declares that he will sing unto the Lord because when all is said and done he knows God always deals bountifully with him. He knows God gives him all he needs. No matter what the problem is David's trust and confidence is always in God.

Prayer:

Father, though I sometimes feel as though my answer is not coming and I feel as if you have not heard me, I know you hear

me and I know you promised when I call that You will Answer. I will not be moved by the enemy. I will not let thoughts of defeat prevail, but I believe in your promise that you will cause me to triumph in Christ Jesus. I rise above my feelings; I rise above the problems and declare my trust and confidence is in You Lord. I will rejoice in your salvation. I will sing and rejoice always because you have dealt abundantly with me. According to Your Word Oh Lord, I have all I need; generous and plentiful blessings so I will not lose sleep; I will not die but live to rejoice in you for your provision. My confidence is in your mercy and loving-kindness. I thank you oh Lord my God and Father for Your goodness and mercy that endures forever. Even before I see the answer I will sing and rejoice for all your provision. In Jesus' Name I pray.

The Psalms are so inspiring. They are actually petitions and supplications David made to God and many times you will see that God answered David by speaking through David's own heart.

"Praise ye the LORD. Blessed is the man that feareth the LORD, that delighteth greatly in his commandments. His seed shall be mighty upon earth: the generation of the upright shall be blessed. Wealth and riches shall be in his house: and his righteousness endureth forever. Unto the upright there ariseth light in the darkness: he is gracious, and full of compassion, and righteous. A good man showeth favor, and lendeth: he will guide his affairs with discretion. Surely he shall not be moved forever: the righteous shall be in everlasting remembrance. He shall not be afraid of evil tidings: his heart is fixed, trusting in the LORD. His heart is established, he shall not be afraid, until he see his desire upon his enemies. He hath dispersed, he hath given to the poor; his righteousness endureth for ever; his horn shall be exalted with honor. The wicked shall see it, and be grieved; he shall gnash with his teeth, and melt away: the desire of the wicked shall perish." (Psalm 112 KJV)

Another example of prayer based on the revelation of God's provision and protection is found in Psalm 112.

Prayer:

Heavenly Father, I reverently worship, respect and honor you. My heart is fixed on your Word. I have faith in you and I trust you Lord. I will not fear because my confidence is in you. I praise you Lord for bringing to pass all that I need. You are gracious to cause the light to shine in the dark places because you are full of compassion and righteousness. I have favor with you Lord and my heart is established and fixed on you. I will honor you by living right and by giving to the poor and

reaching out to others. My seed will be mighty on the earth and the blessing of God will be on them for generations to come. All my needs are met according to your riches in glory by Christ Jesus. My enemies will see the blessings of God upon my life and their desire and plan for evil against me will perish. No matter what my circumstances may be, I thank you for your promises and my faith is in you. In Jesus' Name I pray. Amen.

DO EVERYTHING AS UNTO THE LORD

I n all we do we must remember to do it with all our hearts; we must do everything just as if we were doing it for the Lord and not for men. Colossians 3:23-24 reminds us that when we do things as unto the Lord we will receive the reward of our inheritance from Him. Sometimes we forget, but we must remember we are serving the Lord and not man. I'm talking about in our jobs, in our homes for our family, for our friends, for our church. Whatever we do, let us do it as unto the Lord. Though we get our paycheck from our employer or favor from our friends, family and more, it is ultimately God our Father who rewards us and grants us what we need. What we do for others willingly and as unto the Lord and in the Name of Jesus will be blessed.

Prayer:

Father, in the Name of Jesus, I commit to serve you and only you. Whatever I do I do it as unto you. Whatever my job is, I work at it wholeheartedly; whatever I do throughout my day, I will remember to do it as something done for You Lord and not for men. Because you have promised, I know with all certainty that it is ultimately You Lord – not men – who rewards me. I

have faith to believe and receive. Jesus Christ is the one I serve with all I do and my reward comes from above. Amen!

THE RIGHTEOUS SHALL FLOURISH

We are again reminded in the following scriptures of God's promises when we put His Word first place and obey Him.

Psalm 92:12-15 – "The righteous shall flourish like the palm tree: he shall grow like a cedar in Lebanon. Those that be planted in the house of the LORD shall flourish (or grow in grace) in the courts of our God. They shall still bring forth fruit in old age; they shall be fat (full of spiritual vitality – Amplified) and flourishing; to show that the LORD is upright: he is my rock, and there is no unrighteousness in him."

Leviticus 26: 3-5 – "If ye walk in my statutes, and keep my commandments, and do them; Then I will give you rain in due season and the land shall yield her increase and the trees of the field shall yield their fruit. And your threshing shall reach unto the vintage, and the vintage shall reach unto the sowing time: and ye shall eat your bread to the full, and dwell in your land safely."

Deuteronomy 8:18 - "But you shall remember the LORD thy God: for it is he that gives you power to get wealth, that he may establish his covenant which he swore unto thy fathers, as it is this day."

Proverbs 8:12 – "I wisdom dwell with prudence, and find out knowledge of witty inventions."

In Psalm 92:14 (Amplified) says they are "growing in grace and they shall still bring forth fruit in old age; they will be full of spiritual vitality." You don't have to quit because of your age. God is never finished with us and neither is He worried about how young we are in years. What He wants is for us to grow to maturity in Him and fulfill what He has called us to do. His "gifts and calling are without repentance" (Romans 11:29) He doesn't change His mind. He is our rock and His blessing upon us is continual.

In Leviticus, as written above, He talks of giving us rain in due season and the land will yield increase and the trees of the field will yield their fruit. In other words, look for the increase. We will be taken care of; as we sow we shall reap of the harvest; we will have all we need and we will dwell in safety. However, we must remember that it is the Lord who gives us power to get wealth so that He may establish His covenant on the earth. (Deuteronomy 8:18) and in Proverbs 8:12 it says He will give us knowledge of witty inventions by His wisdom. I believe He wants to do that so that we will not only be sustained as He promises, but that we will be in a position to sustain the Kingdom of God on the earth so that we may all go forth doing His Will.

Prayer:

Heavenly Father, as I walk in Your ways and keep Your Word and do them, according to Your Promise I am growing in grace. I am full of spiritual vitality and have received grace to bring forth fruit even in old age. I am strong and vital to your kingdom because you are my Rock and my Fortress. Because I walk in your ways and listen to Your Voice, You will rain down from Heaven with your anointing to bring increase in whatever I put my hand to. I will eat to the full of whatever I need and I will dwell in safety because I remember You Lord and put you first in my life. I thank you that you have given me power to get wealth so that your covenant may be established on this earth. I thank You Lord that you see ahead and you give me wisdom and knowledge of good ideas and witty inventions that will not only sustain me, but sustain Your Kingdom. Thank You Lord, in Jesus's Name I pray. Amen!

MARRIAGE

T here is no better way to pray for husbands and wives than by the Word of God. We don't want to pray the problem; we don't want to tear down what God wants to build up. The words in Ephesians 5:25 – 33 are so plain and clear that I have taken them as the prayer we need to pray first of all for husbands, and then for the wives. God's Word will not return to Him void, (Is. 55:11) isn't that what He said? Then we must believe Him! Whether you are married or looking to get married these prayers will put you in a place to receive from your Heavenly Father.

Prayer for husband

I declare before God and because I believe His Word that my husband loves me as Christ loves the church. He gives himself for me to take care of me emotionally, physically, and in all ways as Christ did for the church, the Body of Christ. My husband loves me as he loves his own body. He nourishes and cherishes me even as the Lord does with the church. He puts the Word of God first place in His life. Father I thank you that your

word will not return void but will accomplish what it is being sent to do. In Jesus' Name I pray. Amen.

Prayer for wife or wife's commitment:

As a wife, Lord I commit to walk in Your Word and to always show love and respect for my husband; to regard, honor, esteem, admire and love him and leave Him in Your hands, not trying to do the work in him that you want to do. I will walk in love to the honor and glory of God. I will be the helpmate you've created me to be. In Jesus' Name I pray. Amen!

LOVE IS THE KEY

W alking in love is covered in 1 Corinthians 13:4 – 8 (Amplified). It deals with so many areas where we may need to pray. If we have wrong feelings toward someone or they have them toward us, or we have a problem forgiving, this "love" chapter covers it all. I like to pray it not only for people that need it but first for myself. Also in Matthew 5:44-45 Jesus tells us to "love our enemies, bless them that curse us and do good to them that hate us and pray for them which despitefully use us and persecute us." This is a big commandment, but Jesus went on to say that when we do these things, we are demonstrating to all that we are the children of our Father in Heaven. Don't you think our Father knows what we are going through? He desires for His family to reach the world and can only do it when the evidence of the Love of God to others is displayed. Love is the key and if we don't have love, we have nothing. (1 Cor. 13:3) It is a big responsibility to live up to, but with God's help and His Word, which we are totally depending on, we can see results. Again, we pray directly from the Bible; filling in the name or names as needed.

Prayer:

According to Your Word, love is the key therefore I pray, _____ is patient and kind, he/she is never envious nor boils over with jealousy, he/she is not boastful, he/she is not haughty and is not conceited or arrogant and inflated with pride. He/she is not rude and does not act unbecomingly. He/she does not insist on his/her own rights or own way, he/she is not self-seeking. He/she is not touchy, fretful or resentful. _____ takes no account of the evil done to him/her and (pays no attention to a suffered wrong). _____ lets go of the evil done to him/her. He/she forgives, shakes it off and resists the temptation to get revenge without God. _____ chooses to let go and lets God take care of the evil done to him/her. He/she does not rejoice at injustice and unrighteousness, but rejoices when right and truth prevail. _____ bears up under anything and everything that comes because of the Love of God. _____ is ever ready to believe the best of every person. His/her hopes are fadeless under all circumstances and endures everything without weakening. Love never fails in _____ because he/she (by faith I believe) puts the Word of God and the Love of God first in everything. Thank You Lord Jesus. Amen.

SALVATION & SPIRITUAL GROWTH

※

A nother perfect prayer you can pray directly from the scripture is in Ephesians 1:16-19 (Amplified). You pray in faith, believing God's will in the situation. Just fill in the name or names of the people you are praying for and believe God. We can pray for the wisdom and revelation of the knowledge of God to be revealed to us or to whomever you need to pray for. Instead of talking about how bad this person is or how they don't understand certain things, you can pray in faith, believing that God will bring revelation and understanding to them. We don't need to know how, we don't need to be the one to preach it to them; we need to be the one that asks of God and He will bring it to pass!! Don't let doubt and unbelief cloud your prayer regarding the person you are praying for. Yes, the scripture in Deuteronomy 30:19 says there is a choice to be made. People are making choices all day long; some for good and some for evil. In view of this fact, we realize that the person we are praying for has to make the choice to respond to God, but we can still make the choice to pray for them and ask on their behalf and leave them in the hands of God. I believe as He said, His Word will not return to Him void but it will accomplish what it is being sent to do; it's in His time, not ours. So let us be patient and believe what we cannot see, trusting God for the outcome.

Prayer:

Father, I pray that you will grant to _____ a spirit of wisdom and revelation of a deep and intimate knowledge of our Lord Jesus Christ. That _____ will have the eyes of his/her heart flooded with light so that he/she can know and understand the hope to which God through our Lord Jesus has called him/her and how rich our Lord's glorious inheritance is to him/her. I pray that _____ will know and understand what the immeasurable and unlimited and surpassing greatness of God's power is to him/her and all those who believe. In Jesus' Name I pray. Amen.

SALVATION FOR OUR HOUSEHOLD

❄

There are those in your household that need salvation. When it comes to your family you can declare along with Joshua, "as for me and my house, we will serve the Lord." (Joshua 24:14) And you can believe God that there will be someone, if not you, that will be able to reach them with the Gospel....someone will cross their path that they will listen to. Sometimes our family is immune to us; they stop hearing us. But God never stops hearing our prayers and He wants us and our household to be saved and serving Him. So we have God on our side and with Him on our side we cannot lose if we follow His will and His way of doing things.

I am reminded of a story my Mom tells about her father, (my grandfather) and how he told bible stories to her and her siblings and read the Bible to them. It was at a time when his religion was not accepting of a lay person reading the Bible and telling stories from it. He suffered persecution for that and more, but he is the one who prayed for us and I am grateful to God that he did. Though he is already in heaven, his prayers for his family are still being answered today. So don't give up on your family!

From the Old Testament till now God has promised us that if we keep His ways, not only our children but our children's children will be blessed in generations to come. He promised that our days will be prolonged that we will live long and have a life worth living. (Proverbs 3:2 Amp) That's important, to have a life worth living, and that is exactly what our Father in heaven wants for us. He doesn't want us dragging ourselves from day to day only looking for the day we die so we can be with the Lord and not have our problems anymore. He wants us to have a long life and a life worth living and we cannot do that without Him!! There are many scriptures that promise that if we make known the commandments of the Lord and his wonderful works that our children and generations to come will "set their hope in God and will not forget the works of God but will keep His commandments." (Psalm 78:6-7)

Prayer:

Father, I am asking for those of my household to be saved and that they serve you, Lord, all the days of their lives. I pray that they will confess with their mouth that Jesus is Lord and that they believe in their heart that God has raised Him from the dead; for with their heart they believe unto righteousness and with their mouth confession is made unto salvation. (Romans 10:9-10) I thank you Lord that my family has received Christ as their Savior; I thank you that they are living for Him and serving Him all the days of their lives. I thank you that they are disciples well taught of the Lord and great is their peace and

undisturbed composure, (Isaiah 54:13 Amplified) that they put the Word of God first place in their lives, and because of that, they will have a long life and a life worth living. I thank you that they stand AGAINST what they know is wrong and they stand FOR what they know is right. My children and generations to come will set their hope in God and not forget the works of God but will keep His commandments. In Jesus' Name I pray. Amen!

The book of Ephesians is so full of prayers and instructions on how we should live for God. Paul prayed continually and he left his examples in the Bible for us to learn. In chapter 3:16-19, we again find a prayer we can pray in faith for the spiritual growth of those that God has laid upon our hearts.

Prayer:

Father I pray that you grant to _____ out of the rich treasury of Your glory that he/she will be strengthened and re-inforced with mighty power in the inner man by the Holy Spirit Himself indwelling in his/her innermost being and personality. May Christ through our faith dwell, abide and make His per-manent home in _____ heart. May he/she be rooted deep in love and founded securely on love. I pray that _____ may have the power and be strong to apprehend and grasp

what is the breadth and length and height and depth of the love of Christ which far surpasses knowledge or experience. I pray that _____ will be filled with all the fullness of God and the peace of God that passes all understanding. In Jesus Christ our Lord I pray. Amen!

CALLED TO GOD'S SERVICE

M any feel the call to God's service and they should. When we received Christ as our Savior and Lord, we were made the righteousness of God in Christ. We have committed our lives to the Lord and we feel the call on our hearts to obey the great commission to reach the people with the message of salvation and all of His blessings. This is not just for ministers; this is for all believers. We have all been given the ministry of reconciliation....to let others know that God has bridged the gap and they can be reconnected with their Heavenly Father and for them to know that He wants to bless them. Since the fall of Adam we have been disconnected but God has done a great miracle and bought us back to Him through our Lord Jesus Christ. Our vocation is the divine calling of God to walk worthy of Him, letting Him be our example in all things. We are ambassadors; we represent the Lord Jesus Christ on this earth.

Ephesians 4:1 (Amplified) – "I THEREFORE, the prisoner for the Lord, appeal to and beg you to walk (lead a life) worthy of the [divine] calling to which you have been called [with behavior that is a credit to the summons to God's service]."

Let us take heed to the scripture in Ephesians 4:1 (Amplified) as we pray the following prayer.

Prayer:

Father I pray that _____ will walk and lead a life worthy of the divine calling to which he/she has been called and that it will be with behavior that is a credit to the summons to God's service. He/she will not shrink back but will respond to the wooing of the Holy Spirit to do all that pleases You, Lord. I believe Your Word and I believe that Your Word will not return to you void. In Jesus' Name I pray Amen.

COMMITMENT TO LOVE AND SERVE HIM

❊

E phesians 6:19- 20 (Amplified) "And [pray] also for me, that [freedom of] utterance may be given me, that I may open my mouth to proclaim boldly the mystery of the good news (the Gospel), for which I am an ambassador..."

Prayer:

Father, in Jesus' Name I pray also that not only will I walk and lead a life worthy of the divine calling to which I have been called and that it will be with behavior that is a credit to the summons to God's service, but I pray that freedom of utterance will be given to me that I may open my mouth to proclaim boldly the mystery of the Gospel of the Lord Jesus Christ whose Ambassador I am and whom I serve. Amen

PROSPER AND BE IN HEALTH

⁂

I n 3 John 1:2-4 the Apostle John states in verse 4 that he has no greater joy than to hear that his children, those he has taught, are living their lives in the Truth. So I want to also pray that same prayer for my children and all those that I have reached with the gospel. It is preceded by the prayer in verse 2 where John prays that "our health would prosper even as our soul (mind, will, emotions, reasoning and thinking faculties) prosper." So as we renew our minds by study, meditation and praying God's Holy Word for every situation, we will see results in our family, our friends and everyone we are praying for.

Prayer:

Thank you Lord that my children and all those I have shared the gospel with are living their lives in the Truth of Your Word and that they are prospering in every way in their spirit, soul and body. That you cause them to prosper and be in health as their soul prospers. They are disciples well taught of the Lord and great is their peace and undisturbed composure. I thank You Lord that they live their lives giving service to the brethren

and especially to the strangers in our midst. Thank you Lord that they live according to your Word. That they honor Father and Mother that it may be well with them and they obey Your Word so that they will have a long life and a life worth living. Amen.

HEALING AND WELLNESS

W hile healing and receiving healing is another whole subject, never to be exhausted except when we get to heaven and are able to find out the whole story, I will give some key scriptures for you to study and believe God for healing. The first thing you have to know is that it is God's will to heal you. Don't listen to unbelievers, listen to the Holy Spirit; read and study the Word of God. You must believe God. He is the giver of every good and perfect gift and healing and wellness is a good and perfect gift. He's not trying to teach you a lesson by your illness or anything else you are going through. Yes, we can learn from them and we must, but that is not God's best way. Even if I was given a death sentence, I would want to go to the end with God on my side, walking me through. And through it all I want to believe God's Word, believe Him and believe He will do it. Put the Word of God first, speak to the symptoms and remind the devil that every name must bow to the Lord Jesus Christ. I'm not telling you not to go to the doctors...Do what you must, but please DO NOT leave God out of your situation!

In Mark 16:15-20 Jesus gave us the great commission to go and preach to the world, to every creature, and to those who believe, they will be baptized, they will be saved, they will have signs following them as they share with others. Those signs will follow all who believe. Jesus said, "In my name you shall cast out devils, you shall speak with new tongues, they shall take up serpents and if they drink any deadly thing it will not hurt them and THEY WILL LAY HANDS ON THE SICK AND THEY SHALL RECOVER."

I am not one who will ignore any portion of scripture unless I am waiting on God to reveal its meaning to me. So even though we are discussing prayer and praying God's Word, for a moment I want to discuss the portion of scripture that mentions taking up serpents and drinking any deadly thing. The Lord is not telling us to take up serpents and drink deadly things. These are not something you should do to prove you are a Christian and believing God. All will know we are Christians by our love! The lesson here is that Paul shows us in the book of Acts (28:3-6), that when a deadly serpent attached itself to Paul, he just shook it off and kept going. There are other historical facts of unbelievers trying to poison the messenger of the gospel and the messenger of the gospel survived. So this is an area of protection from the Lord that we should grab a hold of and believe Him. We don't do these things on purpose, but as we go we can believe for God's divine protection while we are ministering the gospel to all. We can believe God for healings, miracles, signs and wonders to be performed through us as we yield to the Holy Spirit, but we don't have to handle snakes or drink poison to prove anything. God is the proof! His love is the proof! His blessings are the proof!

Isaiah 53:4-5 tells us that "surely he has borne our griefs, carried our sorrows...that He was wounded for our transgressions, he was bruised for our iniquities and the punishment of our peace was upon Him and by His stripes we are healed." Peter also quoted this scripture in 1 Peter 2:24 "...by whose (Jesus') stripes you were (already) healed." These scriptures speak of being delivered from grief and sorrow, depression that keeps us anxious, and physical illnesses. I want you to take note that those griefs, depression and sorrow can make you ill. So know that He was wounded for all of those things. He was put to death because the people of Jesus' day couldn't believe that God would provide such a One to humanity. It upset their thinking and their way of doing things. Then He was resurrected and appeared to many before leaving this earth, sealing the covenant with His blood anew in heaven before our Father. If you need healing in any of these areas, believe His Word first; put it first; meditate on it day and night. Feed your spirit man with His Holy Word, with praise and worship to Him and He will bring it to pass.

Prayer:

Father, I do believe your word. I believe it is your will to heal me in spirit, soul (my mind, my will and my emotions) and in my body. I refuse to have another down day because of sickness, disease, grief and sorrow. Every name that is named against me

must bow to the Lord Jesus Christ. _____ is a name that must bow to the Name of Jesus. I believe in the Blood Covenant. I believe it is His will for me to be well; to be at peace; to be stress-free and to be delivered. Not only do I believe it, but I receive it now in the mighty Name of Jesus. Amen!

Another wonderful scripture from the Psalms that helps you turn your heart to our Lord in time of distress is Psalm 34.

"I will bless the LORD at all times: his praise shall continually be in my mouth. My soul shall make her boast in the LORD: the humble shall hear thereof, and be glad. O magnify the LORD with me, and let us exalt his name together. I sought the LORD, and he heard me, and delivered me from all my fears. They looked unto him, and were lightened: and their faces were not ashamed. This poor man cried, and the LORD heard him, and saved him out of all his troubles. The angel of the LORD encampeth round about them that fear him, and delivereth them." (Psalm 34:1-7 KJV)

This particular Psalm (the first 4 verses) was also a song we used to sing and it helped me get through a time of depression and fear when I first began my walk with the Lord. I studied this scripture to find many revelations that helped me and I pray now it will help you.

As verse 1 said, I began to praise him at all times, even through tears and suffering. I committed to let the praise of God continually be in my mouth. My soul, which is my mind, my will and my emotions, will make her boast in the Lord. So I praised him through all my troubles. The humble, I learned, are those who are depressed in mind and circumstance, the needy. So this scripture is telling me that those who are needy in mind or circumstance will hear me boasting in the Lord and that they would be glad. Why? Because they can have the same hope, the same comfort that I was experiencing. They saw a way out through the Lord.

Verse 3 says we should magnify the Lord and exalt his name together because, I sought the Lord and he heard me (verse 4). Remember he hears us when we call. He heard me and delivered me out of all my fears. The humble heard me talk of the Lord's deliverance and they looked to the Lord and they were made to be cheerful (lightened) and they were not ashamed or confused. They saw the way. I called to the Lord and he heard me and saved me out of all my troubles and they saw that they could do the same. Isn't this what the gospel is all about; sharing the good news with others?

Verse 7 became a big bonus. "The angel of the Lord encamps around them that fear, reverence and worship the Lord and they delivered them." The angels are here right now surrounding you, waiting for you to praise him at all times and they will not only deliver you but they will join with you in praise to him. I always wondered who David was talking to when he said in verse 3 "O magnify the Lord with me and let us exalt his name together" and now I know it was the angels that encamped around him. So when I sing that song or just read those scriptures I just invite the angels to join me in magnifying his name. O taste and see that the Lord is good (verse 8).

Prayer:

I will bless you Lord at all times; your praise will continually be in my mouth. I will make my boast in you Lord so that others will hear and be glad. I will call upon the angels to join me in praise and worship unto you, Lord, because you are worthy of all my praise; for you have delivered me out of all my fears. I receive and I believe now for my deliverance from all that troubles me in Jesus' Name. Amen

CONCLUSION

T here are so many more scriptures that you can base your prayers on. As you continue in the Word of God, the Holy Spirit will show you how to pray in your particular situation and you will call to Him and He will answer. You will see many great and wonderful things come to pass. Stay in the Word; believe for His revelation as you meditate on it and then act on it.

I want to say to stand still and see the salvation and deliverance of the Lord, but I don't want to mislead you. Many have quoted Exodus 14:13 which says "Fear not, stand still and see the salvation of the Lord..." So many think they should stay put. They pray, quote the Word and don't do anything else; but that's not what He wanted. God is on the GO...Look at just two verses later in verse 15 where the Lord said to Moses, "why are you crying to me? Speak to the children (those he was leading) and tell them to GO FORWARD." Yes, you will see the salvation and deliverance of the Lord, but you can't stay at the brink of the ocean. YOU NEED TO STAND STILL, HEAR FROM HIM, DON'T LOOK BACK, DON'T COMPLAIN AND JUST GO FORWARD. Take that step of faith; don't stand on the brink of disaster; let Him part the sea for you. Verse 16 says to lift up your rod, in this case, the Word of

God. Stretch out your hand over the sea (the problem) and go forth on dry ground towards the land of milk and honey (my paraphrase). Continue in His Word; in Prayer; and in Worship to Him. These things will move you forward in God to receive the blessings you are looking for.

I am extremely attached to certain old songs that we used to sing back in the mid 70's through to the 90's. It seemed that it was a time of great revelation of the Holy Spirit and the anointing. These songs brought the awareness of the Lord to my heart and I loved that we took the songs, especially from the scriptures, and sang them to Him in worship. Rather than to sing about Him; we sang **"to"** Him. This actually was worshipping Him. When I would sing these songs, and they were mostly scripture songs, they brought the presence of God, an anointing that is indescribable, and they brought revelation knowledge of God. Many of the scripture songs that we sing not only teach us the Word, but it gets into our hearts and bolsters our faith. I'm reminded of one of those songs we used to sing years ago:

Ah Lord God, Thou hast made the heavens and the earth by thy great power Ah Lord God, Thou hast made the heavens and the earth by thine outstretched arm. Nothing is too difficult for thee; nothing is too difficult for thee. Great and mighty God, Great in counsel and mighty in deed, mighty in deed. Nothing,

nothing, absolutely nothing, nothing is too difficult for thee. (Jeremiah 32:17)

Indeed it is true; there is nothing too difficult or too hard for him. If you do a word study of the words "outstretched arm" you find that He has His arms stretched out to bless; to make a way; to receive you. He is waiting for you to come to Him. Let this message be a start for you. Look to Him. He loves you with an everlasting love and wants to bless you and take care of you. Don't resist God! I say it again; He loves you; He wants to help you! So run to Him. No matter what your need is, ask of Him according to the Word of God and you shall receive that your joy may be full!

INSTRUCTIONS

M y desire is that this book will become a very personal and private book to you. I have provided the next six pages for you to begin to write your own prayers based on scripture. I feel that it will be helpful to you to have it attached to this book for reference purposes. The blank pages following will be helpful not only for your scriptural prayers but for your own personal thoughts.

Father, I thank you for the person reading this book and now about to put in writing their own prayers based on your Word. I ask you to bless them abundantly, give them the wisdom they need and the peace that passes all understanding to help them get through whatever it is they face in this life. I pray that by Your Holy Spirit they know exactly how to pray in agreement with your Word so that they will receive the results they need. I pray that they will be like a tree planted by the rivers of water, that they will bring forth fruit in its season and, their leaf will not fade or wither and everything they do shall prosper and come to maturity. (Psalm 1:3) I thank you, Father that you hear when they call and you are faithful to answer. In Jesus' Name I pray. Amen!

Scripture: _____

Prayer based on this scripture:

_____

_____

_____

_____

_____

_____

_____

_____

_____

_____

_____

_____

_____

_____

_____

Scripture: _____

Prayer based on this scripture:

_____

_____

_____

_____

_____

_____

_____

_____

_____

_____

_____

_____

_____

_____

_____

_____

Scripture: _____

Prayer based on this scripture:

_____

_____

_____

_____

_____

_____

_____

_____

_____

_____

_____

_____

_____

_____

_____

_____

_____

Scripture: _____

Prayer based on this scripture:

_____

_____

_____

_____

_____

_____

_____

_____

_____

_____

_____

_____

_____

_____

_____

_____

Scripture: _____

Prayer based on this scripture:

_____

_____

_____

_____

_____

_____

_____

_____

_____

_____

_____

_____

_____

_____

_____

_____

_____

Scripture: _____

Prayer based on this scripture:

_____

_____

_____

_____

_____

_____

_____

_____

_____

_____

_____

_____

_____

_____

_____

_____

CPSIA information can be obtained at www.ICGtesting.com
Printed in the USA
LVOW100517230212

269930LV00002B/2/P